My First Origami Book
THINGS THAT GO

Nick Robinson

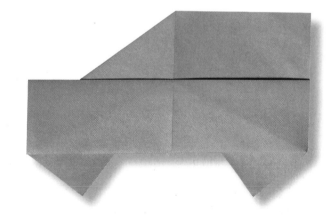

DOVER PUBLICATIONS, INC.
Mineola, New York

GREEN EDITION ®

All designs were created by Nick Robinson, except the Hot Air Balloon (Wayne Brown) the Japanese Glider (Kunihiko Kasahara) and Kite, Van, Helicopter, Jumping Frog, and Rocket which are adapted from traditional designs. Origami designers are constantly creating new simple models—any duplication of existing work is unintentional.

The author would like to thank Jason Schneider and all at Dover for making this book possible. Love to my family: Alison, Daisy, Nick Junior, Matilda, and Ruby. Special thanks to Ros Joyce and Wayne Brown for their assistance. The author can be reached at www.origami.me.uk

Bibliographical Note

My First Origami Book: Things That Go is a new work, first published by Dover Publications, Inc., in 2012.

International Standard Book Number
ISBN-13: 978-0-486-48707-6
ISBN-10: 0-486-48707-5

Manufactured in the United States by Courier Corporation
48707501
www.doverpublications.com

Contents

Kite

This simple shape has enchanted children and adults for centuries. Why not make several of these using different colors, then display them on a board?

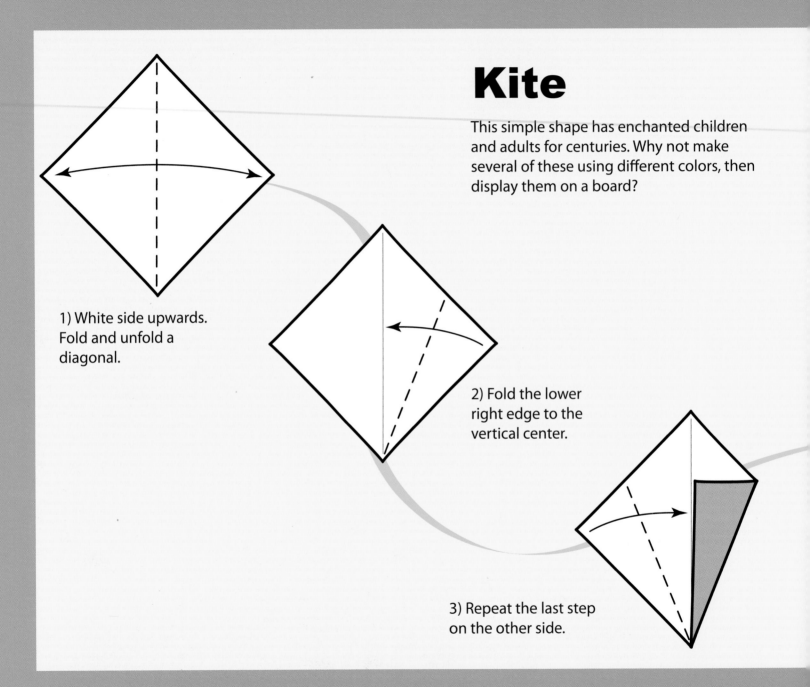

1) White side upwards. Fold and unfold a diagonal.

2) Fold the lower right edge to the vertical center.

3) Repeat the last step on the other side.

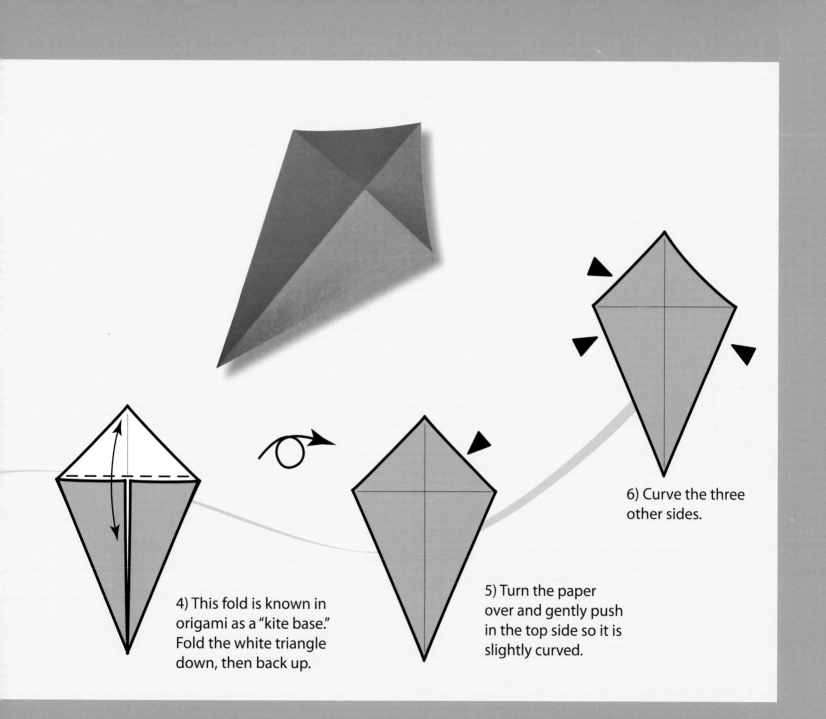

4) This fold is known in origami as a "kite base." Fold the white triangle down, then back up.

5) Turn the paper over and gently push in the top side so it is slightly curved.

6) Curve the three other sides.

Van

The sight of "one man and his van" is common throughout the world. By using different shaped sheets of paper and altering some of the creases, you can create a wide variety of different types of vans.

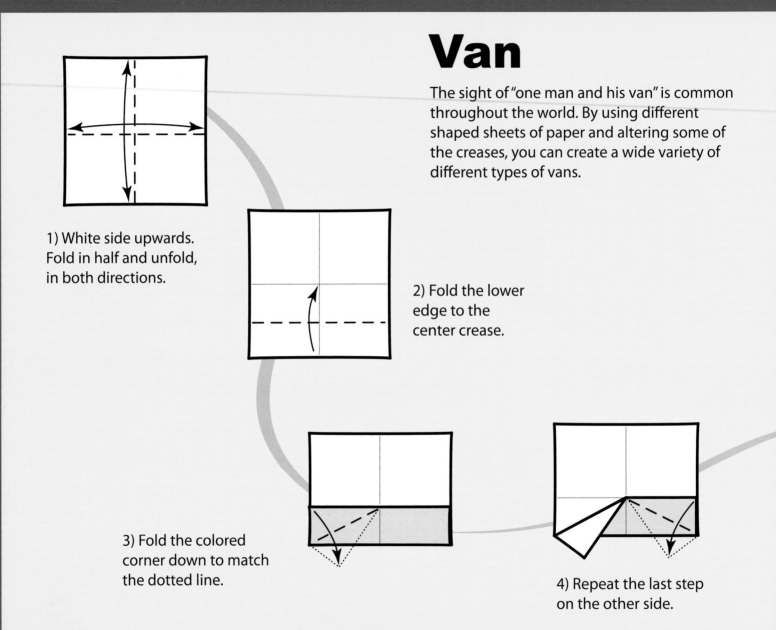

1) White side upwards. Fold in half and unfold, in both directions.

2) Fold the lower edge to the center crease.

3) Fold the colored corner down to match the dotted line.

4) Repeat the last step on the other side.

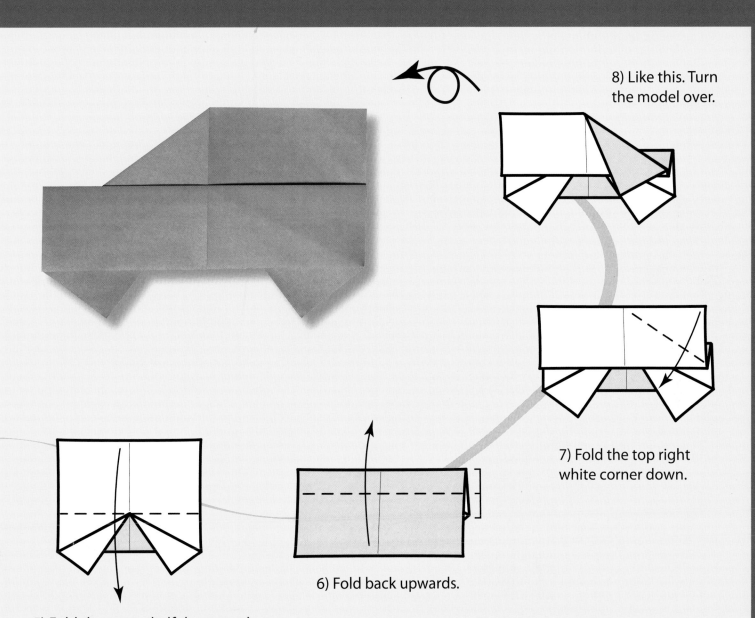

8) Like this. Turn the model over.

7) Fold the top right white corner down.

6) Fold back upwards.

5) Fold the upper half downwards.

Hang Glider

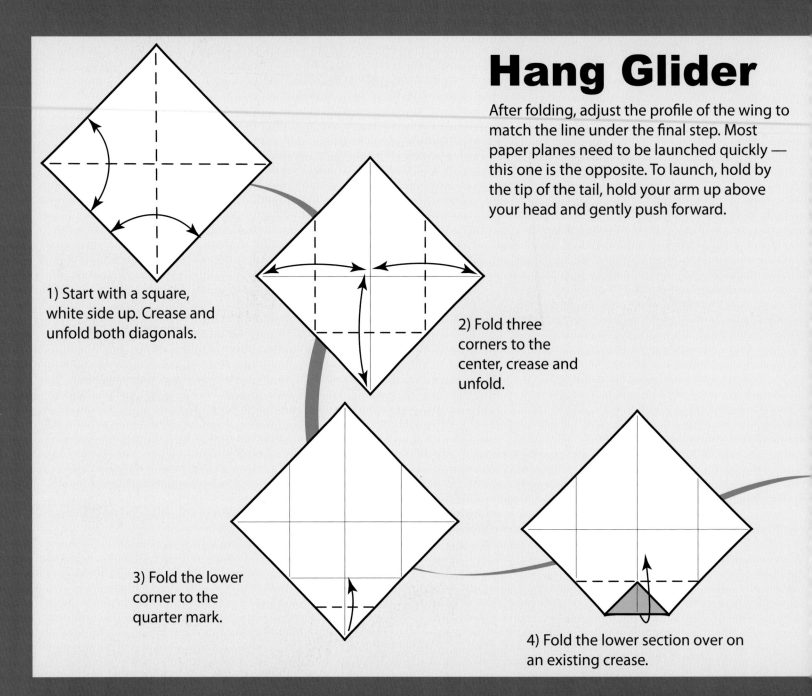

After folding, adjust the profile of the wing to match the line under the final step. Most paper planes need to be launched quickly — this one is the opposite. To launch, hold by the tip of the tail, hold your arm up above your head and gently push forward.

1) Start with a square, white side up. Crease and unfold both diagonals.

2) Fold three corners to the center, crease and unfold.

3) Fold the lower corner to the quarter mark.

4) Fold the lower section over on an existing crease.

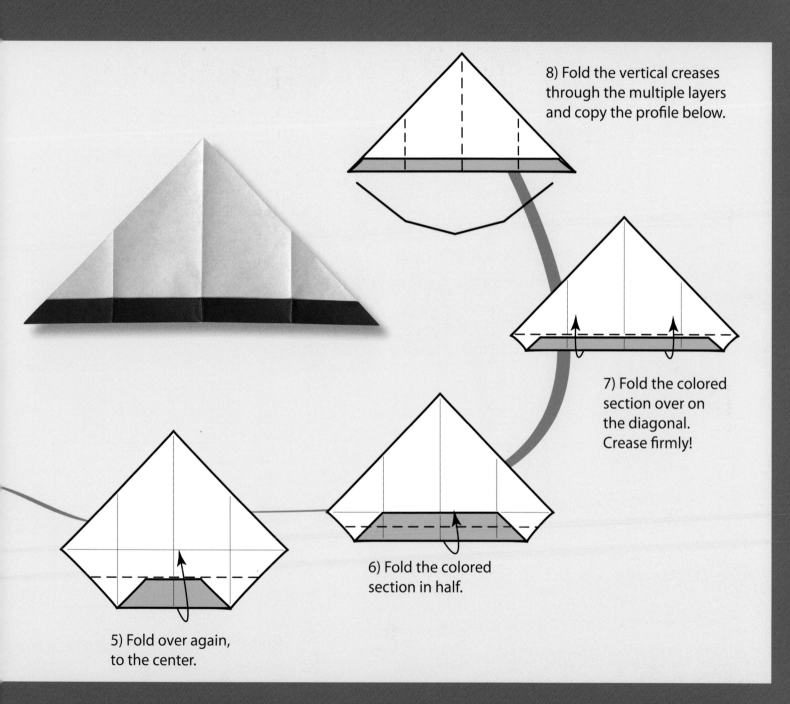

8) Fold the vertical creases through the multiple layers and copy the profile below.

7) Fold the colored section over on the diagonal. Crease firmly!

6) Fold the colored section in half.

5) Fold over again, to the center.

Yacht

This is a perfect design for a greeting card or a wall display. There are many origami yachts, probably because it is such a simple shape. Why not try to create your own design?

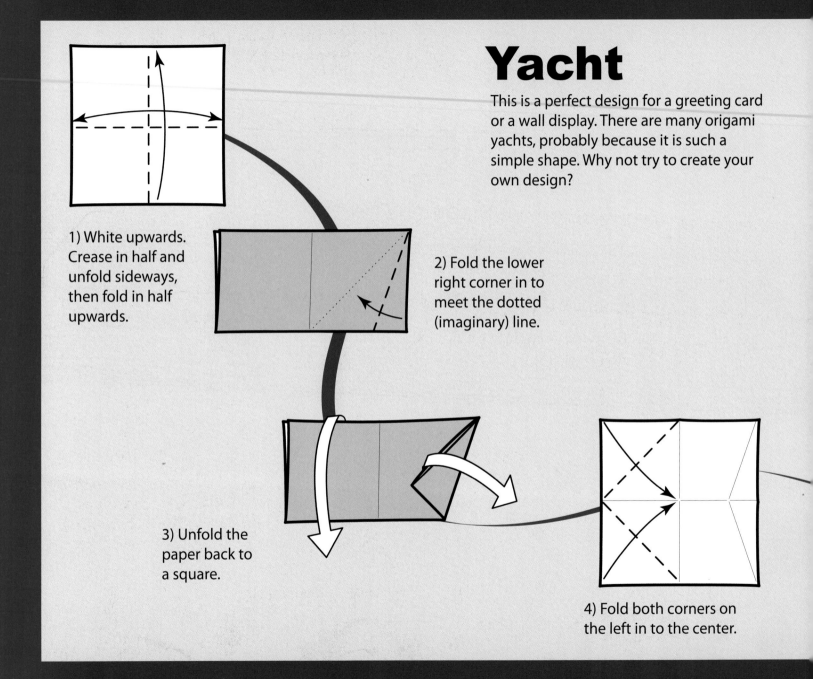

1) White upwards. Crease in half and unfold sideways, then fold in half upwards.

2) Fold the lower right corner in to meet the dotted (imaginary) line.

3) Unfold the paper back to a square.

4) Fold both corners on the left in to the center.

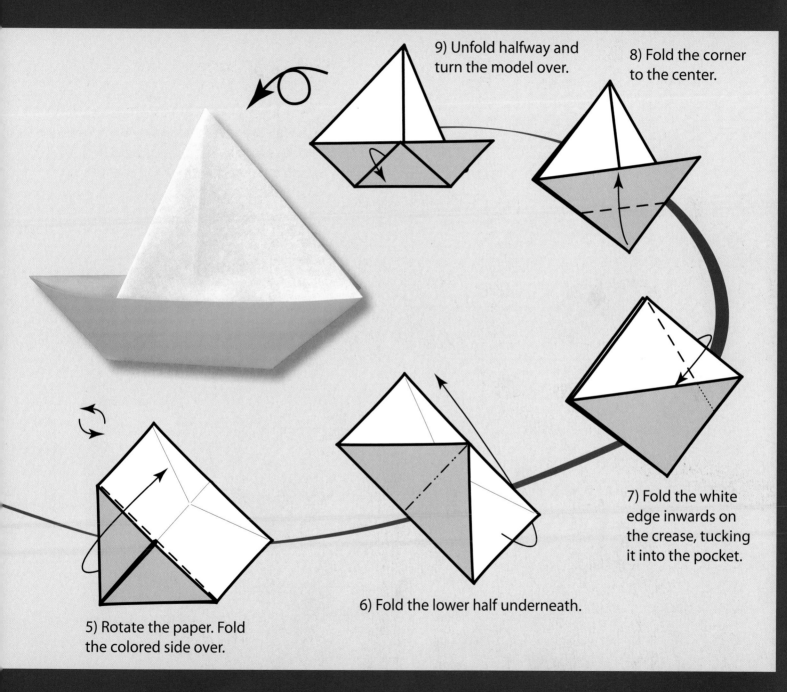

9) Unfold halfway and turn the model over.

8) Fold the corner to the center.

7) Fold the white edge inwards on the crease, tucking it into the pocket.

6) Fold the lower half underneath.

5) Rotate the paper. Fold the colored side over.

Sled

Everyone loves sleds and looks forward to times when there is enough snow to use them. This paper sled will happily slide down a sheet of paper.

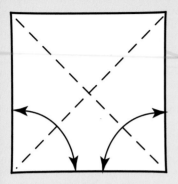

1) White upwards, crease in half corner to corner and unfold, both ways.

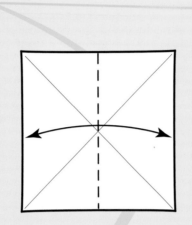

2) Fold in half from side to side, then unfold.

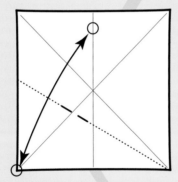

3) Starting the crease at the lower right corner, fold the circled points to meet, but only crease a small amount. Unfold.

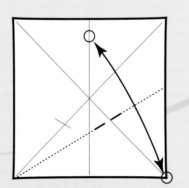

4) Repeat in the opposite direction.

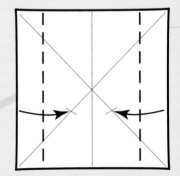

5) Fold the sides in to touch where the creases meet.

10) Make two vertical creases, then unfold half way. Turn the paper over.

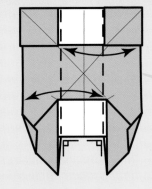

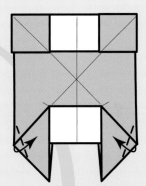

9) Fold two corners inwards a little way.

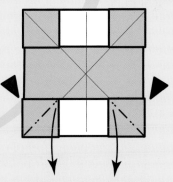

8) Open and squash the triangular flaps.

6) The paper will look like this. Turn the paper over.

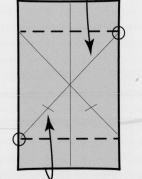

7) Fold the upper edge down and the lower edge up, starting where the diagonal creases meet the edge.

Flat Boat

Many paper boats *look* good, but don't float very well. This design is very stable and you can have races down a stream. If you color the paper with wax crayon before folding, it will stay afloat even longer.

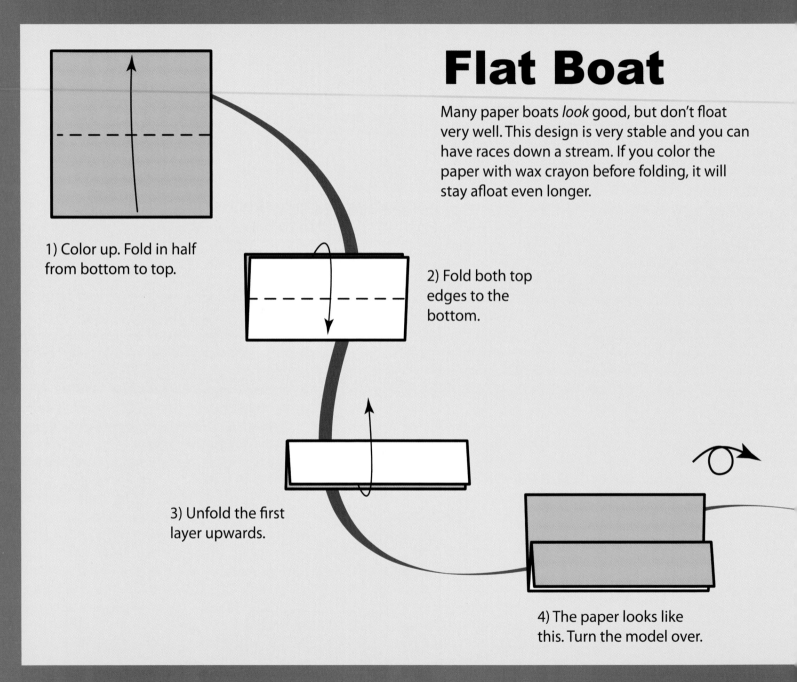

1) Color up. Fold in half from bottom to top.

2) Fold both top edges to the bottom.

3) Unfold the first layer upwards.

4) The paper looks like this. Turn the model over.

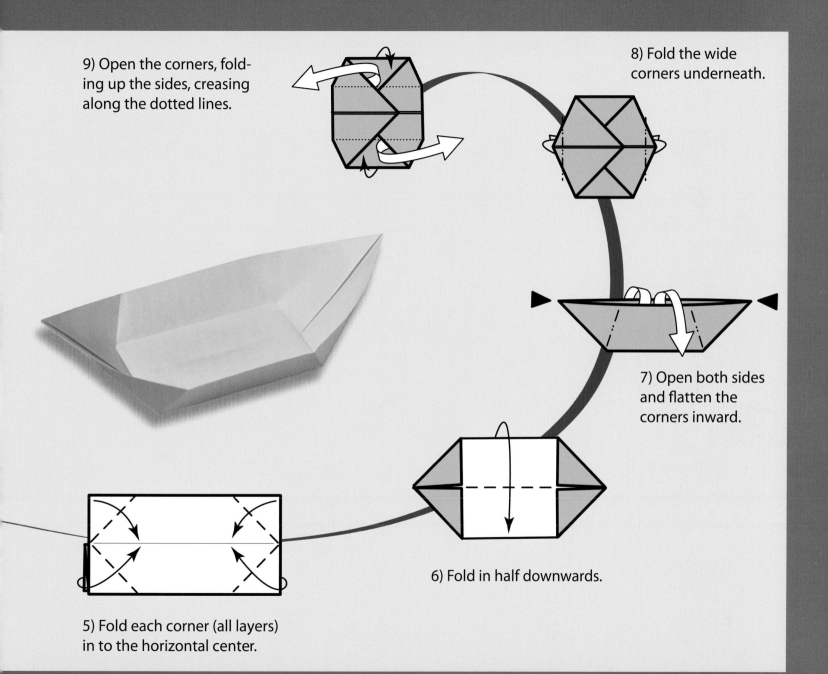

9) Open the corners, folding up the sides, creasing along the dotted lines.

8) Fold the wide corners underneath.

7) Open both sides and flatten the corners inward.

6) Fold in half downwards.

5) Fold each corner (all layers) in to the horizontal center.

UFO

Do UFOs exist? Many people believe they do. This is the classic shape of a UFO but take care at the end when making it 3-D — compare your model with the photo. You can make it fly with a flick of your wrist!

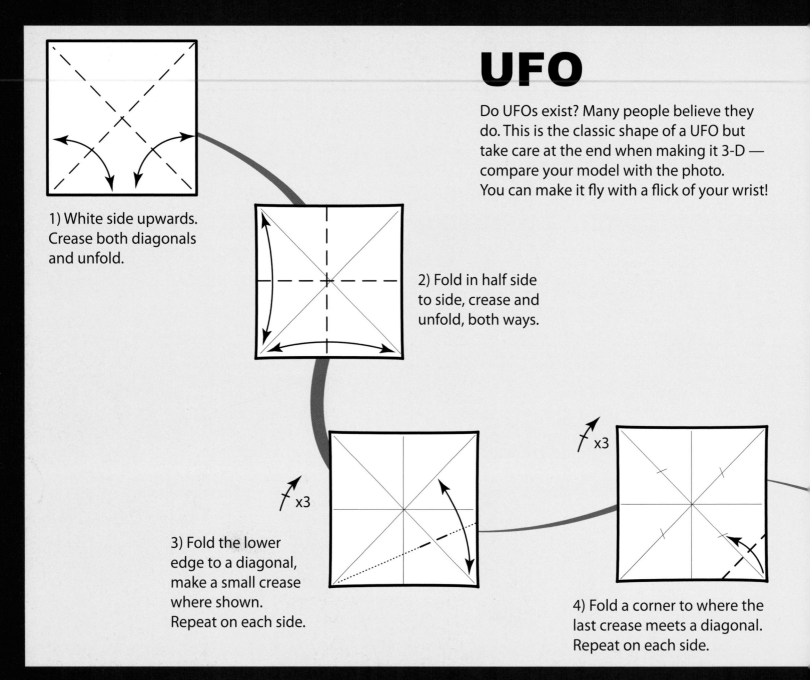

1) White side upwards. Crease both diagonals and unfold.

2) Fold in half side to side, crease and unfold, both ways.

3) Fold the lower edge to a diagonal, make a small crease where shown. Repeat on each side.

4) Fold a corner to where the last crease meets a diagonal. Repeat on each side.

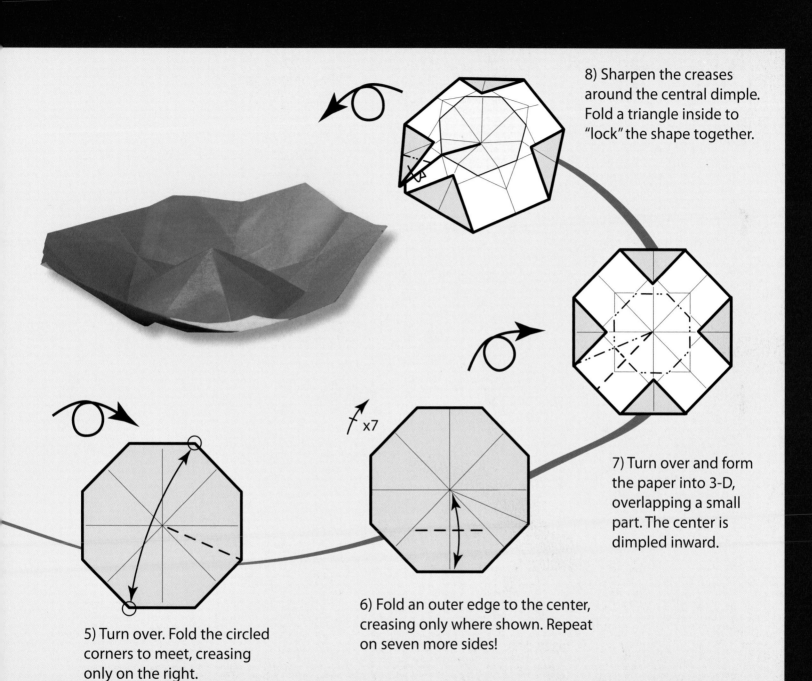

8) Sharpen the creases around the central dimple. Fold a triangle inside to "lock" the shape together.

7) Turn over and form the paper into 3-D, overlapping a small part. The center is dimpled inward.

x7

6) Fold an outer edge to the center, creasing only where shown. Repeat on seven more sides!

5) Turn over. Fold the circled corners to meet, creasing only on the right.

Hot Air Balloon

This model was created by Wayne Brown and needs a 2x1 rectangle. This is easily made by folding a square in half, then cutting along the crease. However, you can experiment with different shaped rectangles for taller or wider balloons.

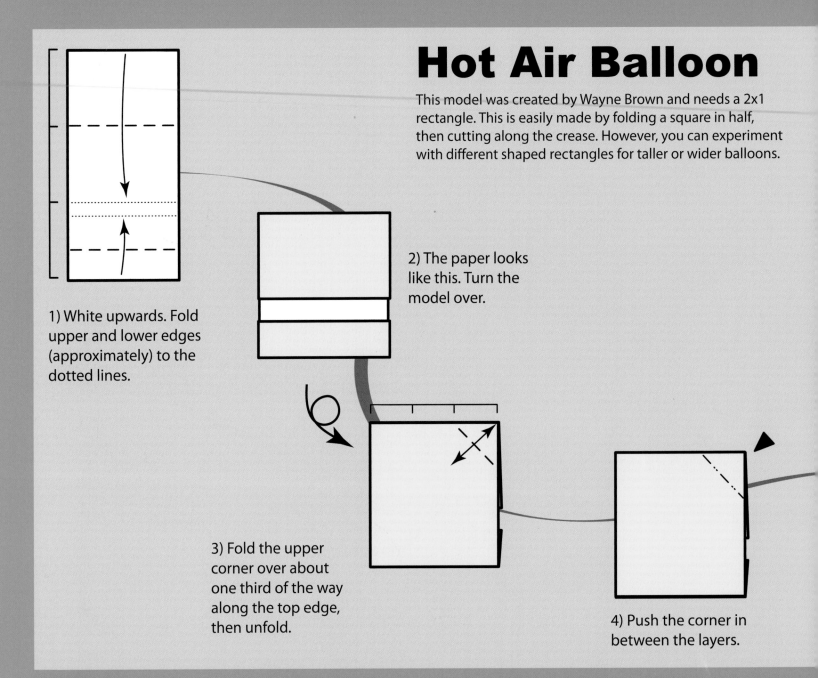

1) White upwards. Fold upper and lower edges (approximately) to the dotted lines.

2) The paper looks like this. Turn the model over.

3) Fold the upper corner over about one third of the way along the top edge, then unfold.

4) Push the corner in between the layers.

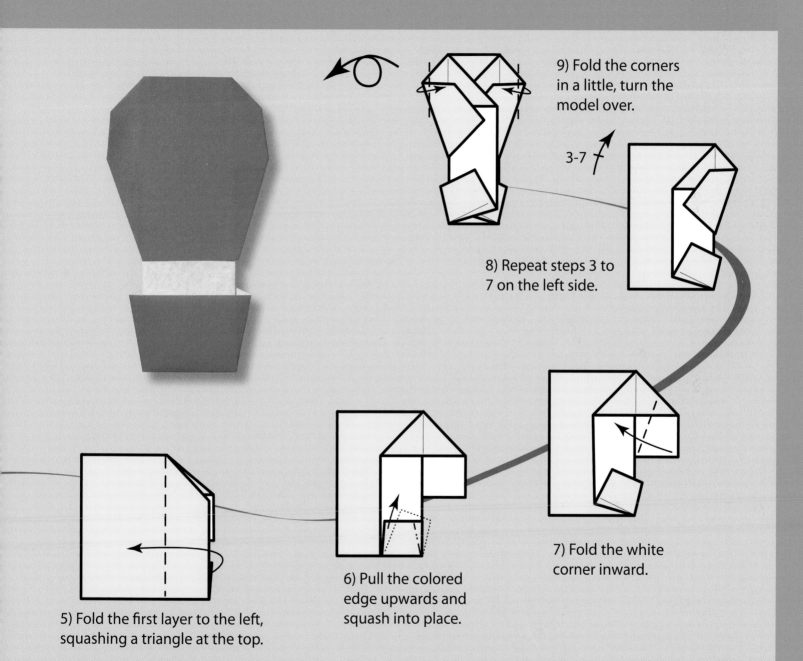

9) Fold the corners in a little, turn the model over.

3-7

8) Repeat steps 3 to 7 on the left side.

7) Fold the white corner inward.

6) Pull the colored edge upwards and squash into place.

5) Fold the first layer to the left, squashing a triangle at the top.

Helicopter

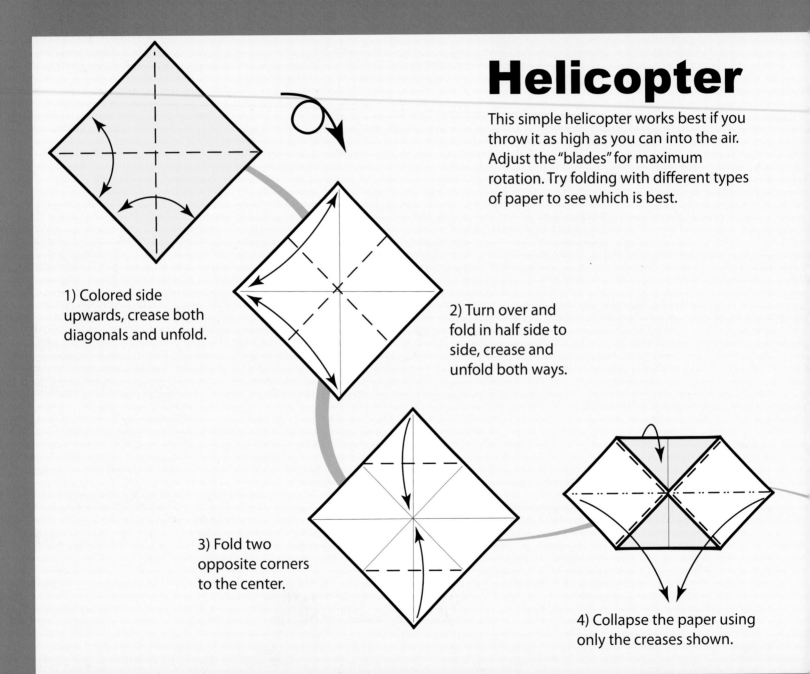

This simple helicopter works best if you throw it as high as you can into the air. Adjust the "blades" for maximum rotation. Try folding with different types of paper to see which is best.

1) Colored side upwards, crease both diagonals and unfold.

2) Turn over and fold in half side to side, crease and unfold both ways.

3) Fold two opposite corners to the center.

4) Collapse the paper using only the creases shown.

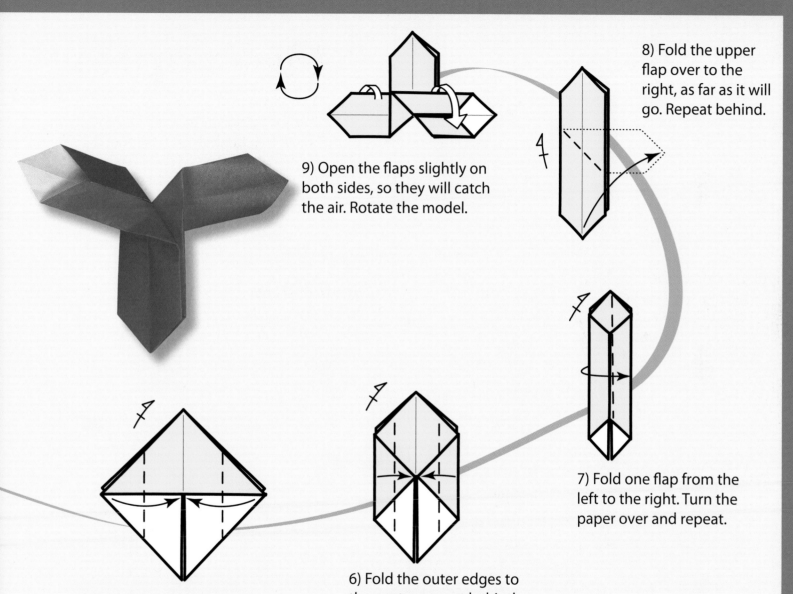

8) Fold the upper flap over to the right, as far as it will go. Repeat behind.

9) Open the flaps slightly on both sides, so they will catch the air. Rotate the model.

7) Fold one flap from the left to the right. Turn the paper over and repeat.

6) Fold the outer edges to the center, repeat behind.

5) Fold the outer corners to the center, repeat behind.

Space Shuttle

It's hard to believe that the age of the Space Shuttle has come to an end, but their exciting take-offs and landings will never be forgotten. What new technology will replace them?

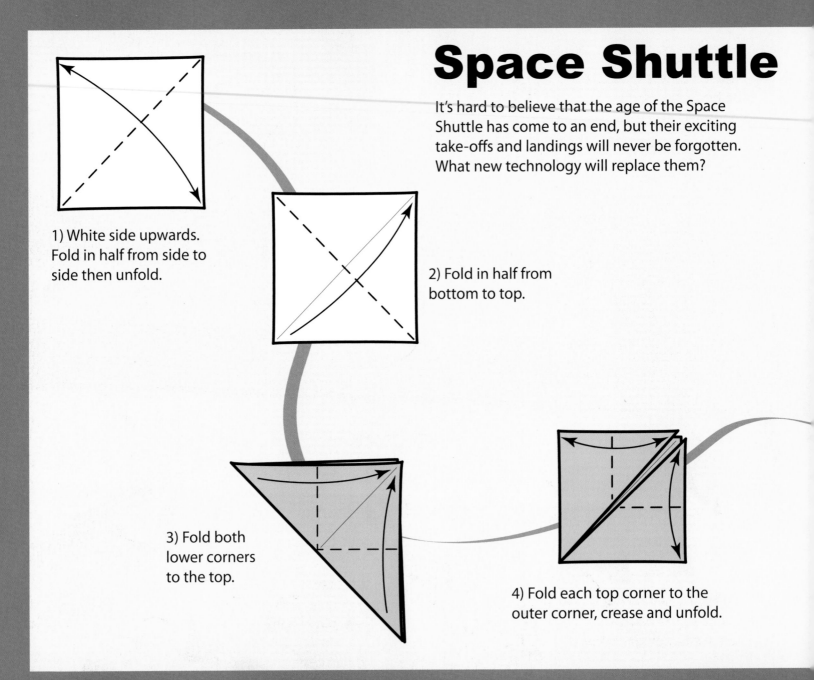

1) White side upwards. Fold in half from side to side then unfold.

2) Fold in half from bottom to top.

3) Fold both lower corners to the top.

4) Fold each top corner to the outer corner, crease and unfold.

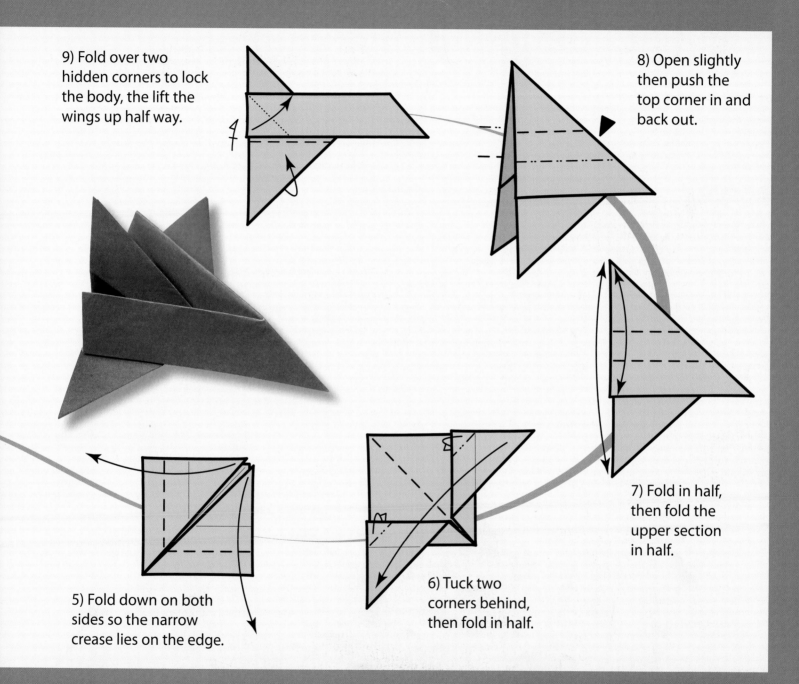

9) Fold over two hidden corners to lock the body, the lift the wings up half way.

8) Open slightly then push the top corner in and back out.

7) Fold in half, then fold the upper section in half.

6) Tuck two corners behind, then fold in half.

5) Fold down on both sides so the narrow crease lies on the edge.

Chariot

This was used to great effect by Roman soldiers. The model itself is a secret until it opens out at the very end. See if you can find an origami horse to pull the chariot!

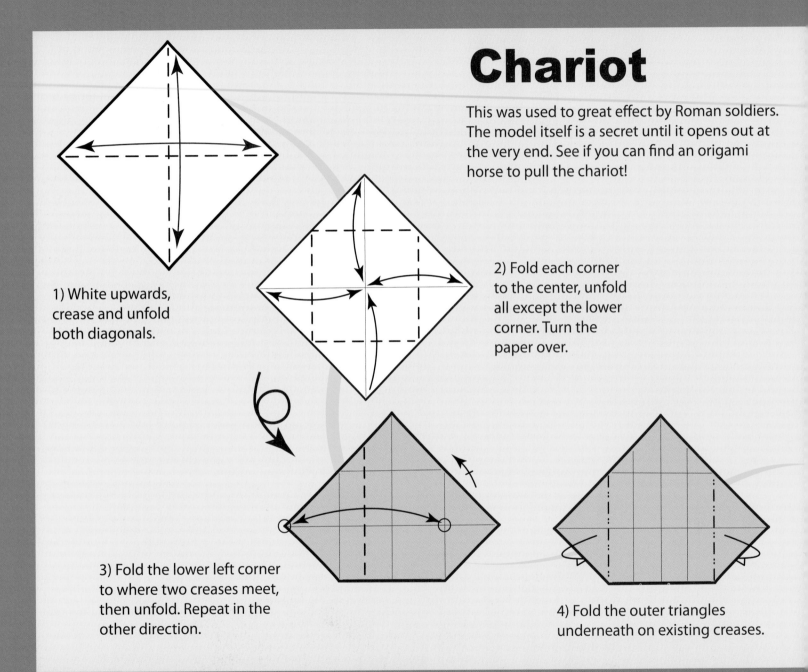

1) White upwards, crease and unfold both diagonals.

2) Fold each corner to the center, unfold all except the lower corner. Turn the paper over.

3) Fold the lower left corner to where two creases meet, then unfold. Repeat in the other direction.

4) Fold the outer triangles underneath on existing creases.

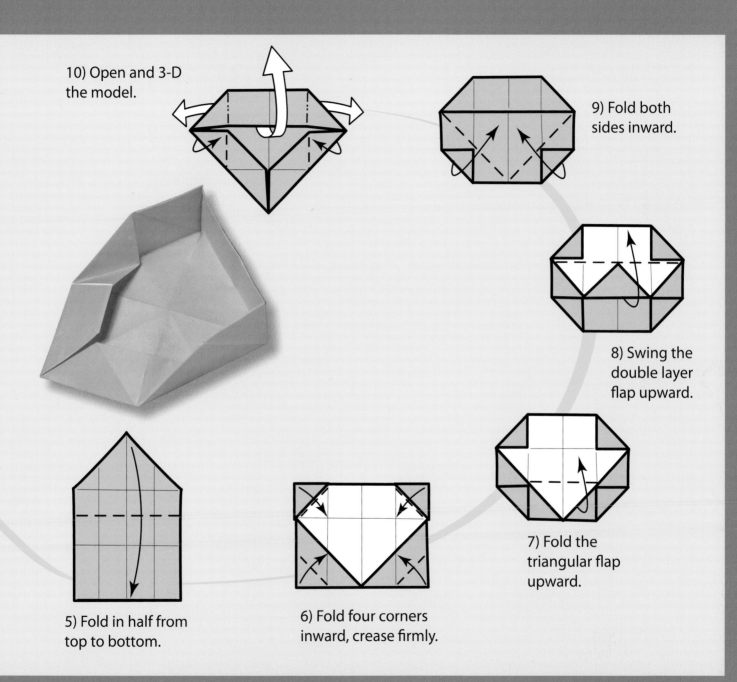

10) Open and 3-D the model.

9) Fold both sides inward.

8) Swing the double layer flap upward.

7) Fold the triangular flap upward.

6) Fold four corners inward, crease firmly.

5) Fold in half from top to bottom.

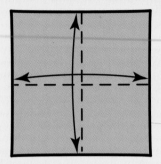

1) Color upwards, crease in half then unfold, in both directions.

Japanese Glider

This design was created by the Japanese Master Kunihiko Kasahara. It is a development of a traditional "house" design. Launch by throwing upwards as high as possible!

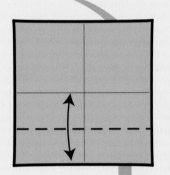

2) Fold the lower edge to the center, crease and unfold.

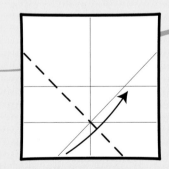

3) Turn the paper over. Make a crease so the circled lines meet, then unfold.

4) Repeat in the other direction.

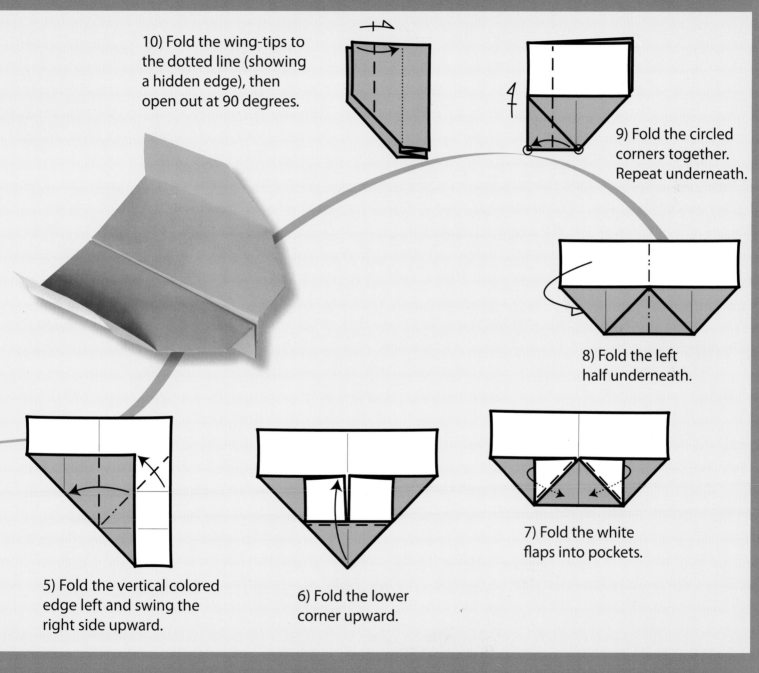

10) Fold the wing-tips to the dotted line (showing a hidden edge), then open out at 90 degrees.

9) Fold the circled corners together. Repeat underneath.

8) Fold the left half underneath.

7) Fold the white flaps into pockets.

5) Fold the vertical colored edge left and swing the right side upward.

6) Fold the lower corner upward.

Speedboat

Speedboats are one of the most exciting forms of transportation. They are the fastest boats on the water. Perhaps a lot of the fun is in the fear you'll fall overboard!

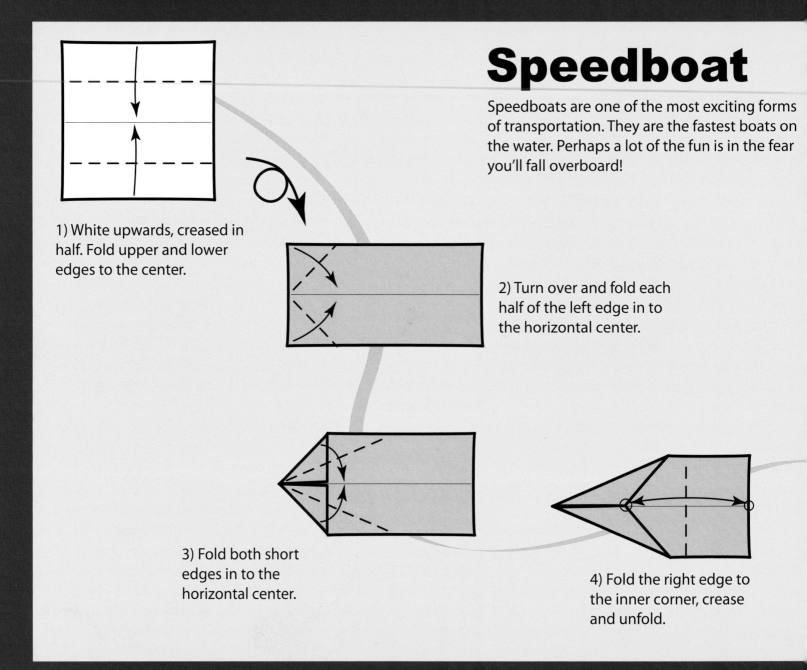

1) White upwards, creased in half. Fold upper and lower edges to the center.

2) Turn over and fold each half of the left edge in to the horizontal center.

3) Fold both short edges in to the horizontal center.

4) Fold the right edge to the inner corner, crease and unfold.

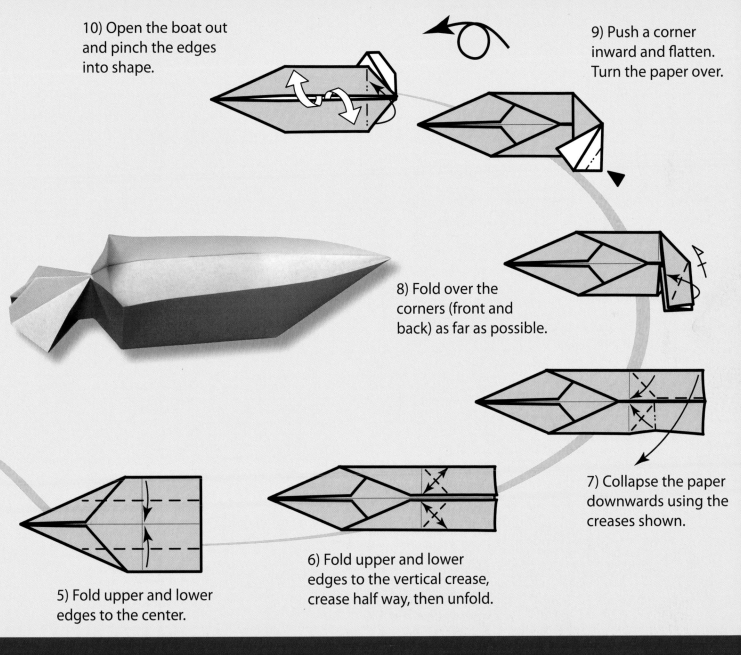

10) Open the boat out and pinch the edges into shape.

9) Push a corner inward and flatten. Turn the paper over.

8) Fold over the corners (front and back) as far as possible.

7) Collapse the paper downwards using the creases shown.

6) Fold upper and lower edges to the vertical crease, crease half way, then unfold.

5) Fold upper and lower edges to the center.

Jumping Frog

Unlike the rest of the models in the book, this is natural rather than man-made, but it certainly "goes!" Press gently down on the zig-zag creases and flick your finger backwards, it will leap forwards! Make the creases in steps 9 and 10 gently, so it will have more spring and jump further.

1) White side upwards, fold in half both ways, crease and unfold.

2) Fold all four corners to the center, unfold two of them.

3) Fold the upper edges over twice.

4) The paper will look like this. Turn the model over.

5) Fold the top corner to the center and turn over again.

30

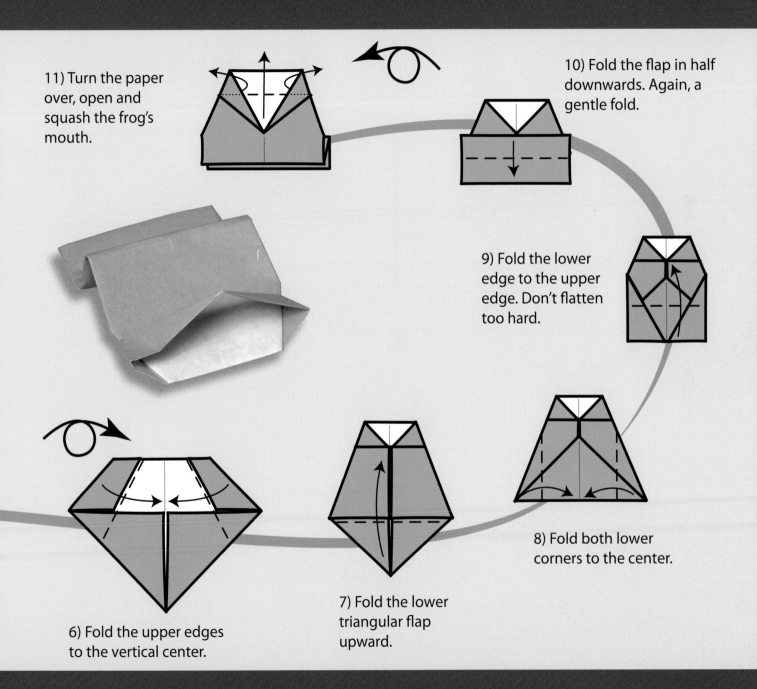

11) Turn the paper over, open and squash the frog's mouth.

10) Fold the flap in half downwards. Again, a gentle fold.

9) Fold the lower edge to the upper edge. Don't flatten too hard.

8) Fold both lower corners to the center.

7) Fold the lower triangular flap upward.

6) Fold the upper edges to the vertical center.

Rocket

Rockets have been used for over 800 years and have developed from crude missiles into sophisticated vehicles, capable of taking men to outer space. This model looks great when folded from foil paper.

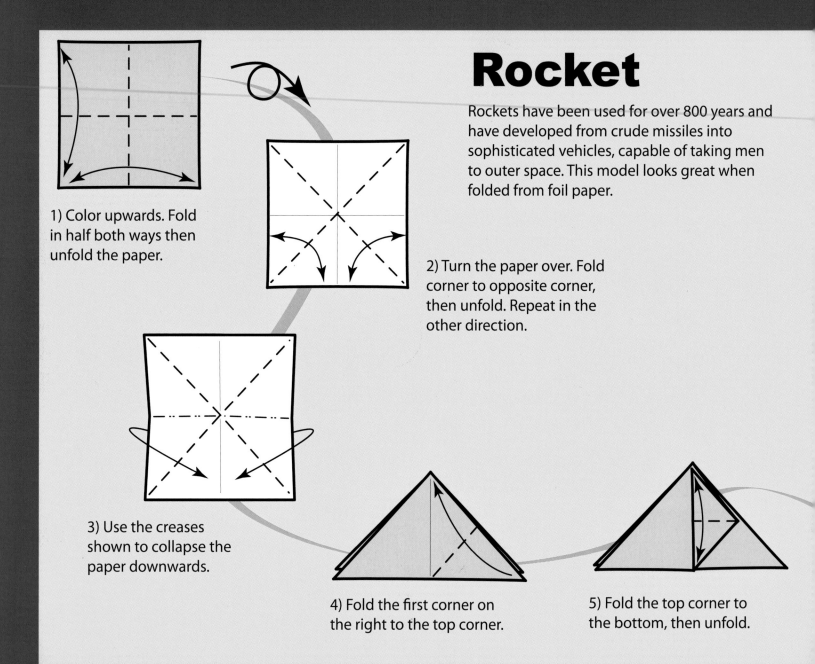

1) Color upwards. Fold in half both ways then unfold the paper.

2) Turn the paper over. Fold corner to opposite corner, then unfold. Repeat in the other direction.

3) Use the creases shown to collapse the paper downwards.

4) Fold the first corner on the right to the top corner.

5) Fold the top corner to the bottom, then unfold.

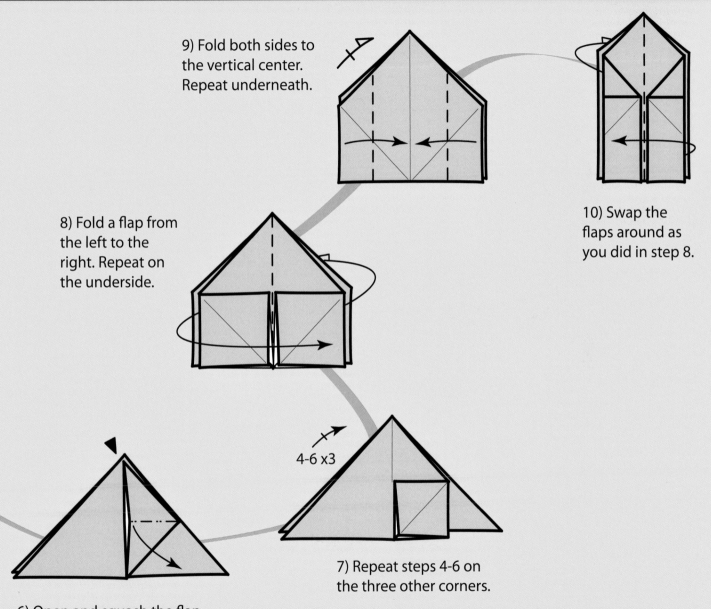

9) Fold both sides to the vertical center. Repeat underneath.

10) Swap the flaps around as you did in step 8.

8) Fold a flap from the left to the right. Repeat on the underside.

4-6 x3

7) Repeat steps 4-6 on the three other corners.

6) Open and squash the flap.

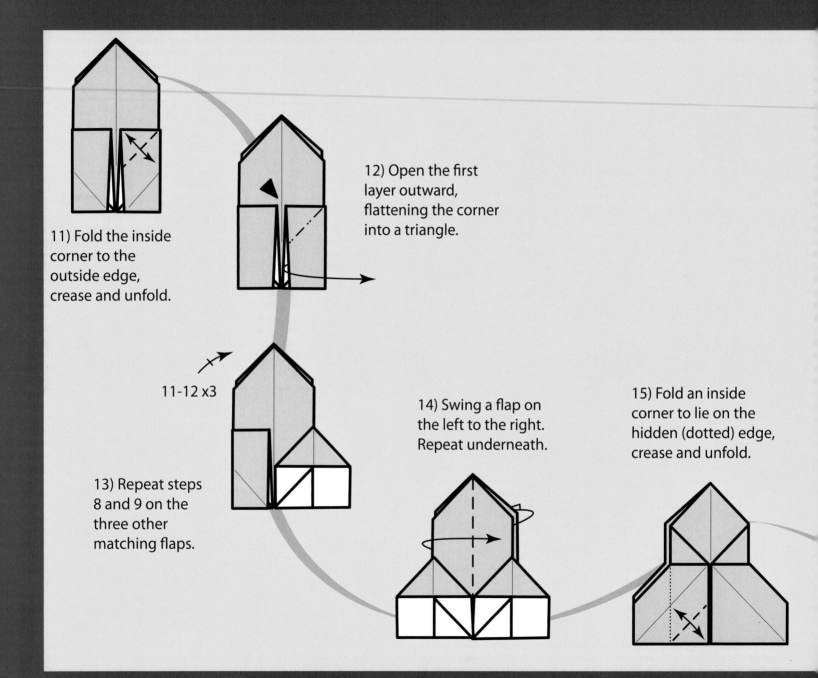

11) Fold the inside corner to the outside edge, crease and unfold.

12) Open the first layer outward, flattening the corner into a triangle.

11-12 x3

13) Repeat steps 8 and 9 on the three other matching flaps.

14) Swing a flap on the left to the right. Repeat underneath.

15) Fold an inside corner to lie on the hidden (dotted) edge, crease and unfold.

20) Open each flap so it is at 90 degrees to the others. It should match the cross shown below.

f x3

19) Fold the white triangle upwards, repeating on the other three flaps.

f x3

12-14 x3

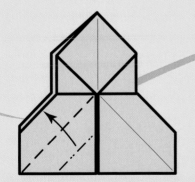

16) Fold over on the valley crease, start to make the mountain crease. Check the next drawing!

18) The paper will look like this. Relax and enjoy the last move, before repeating steps 12-14 on the other three flaps.

17) It's tricky, but stick with it. Follow the arrows and open the middle section into a triangle — see the next drawing!

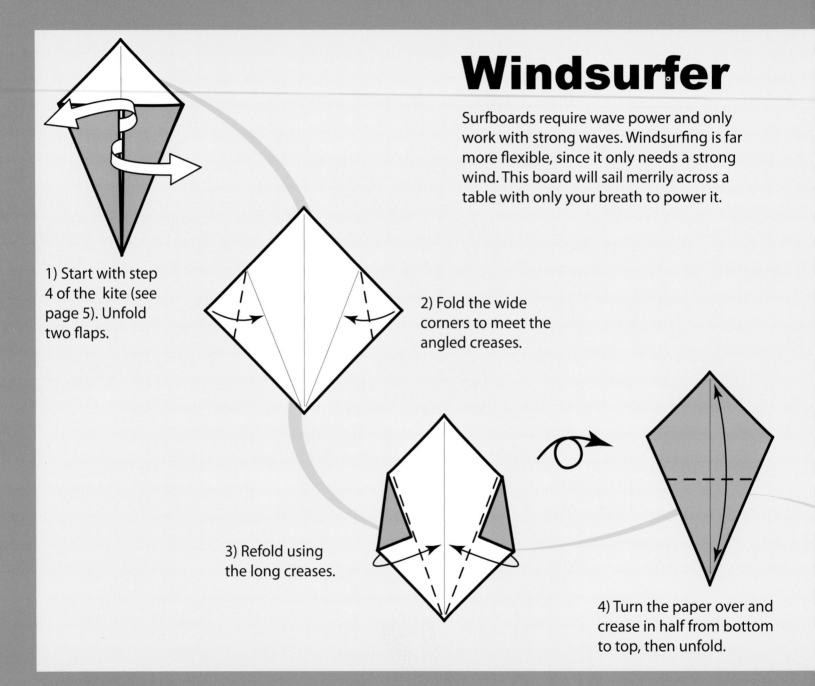

Windsurfer

Surfboards require wave power and only work with strong waves. Windsurfing is far more flexible, since it only needs a strong wind. This board will sail merrily across a table with only your breath to power it.

1) Start with step 4 of the kite (see page 5). Unfold two flaps.

2) Fold the wide corners to meet the angled creases.

3) Refold using the long creases.

4) Turn the paper over and crease in half from bottom to top, then unfold.

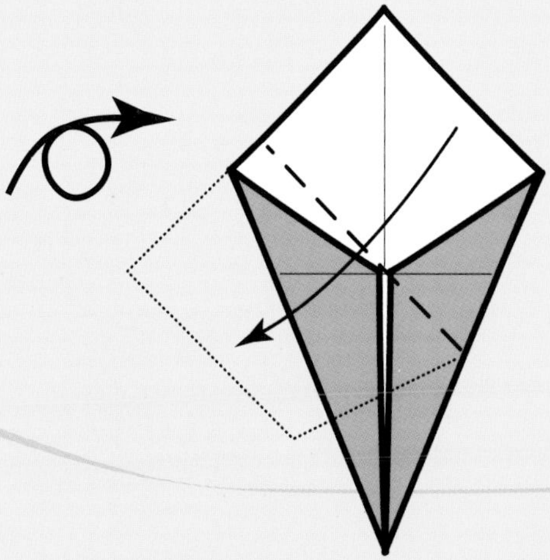

7) Repeat the last move on the other side.

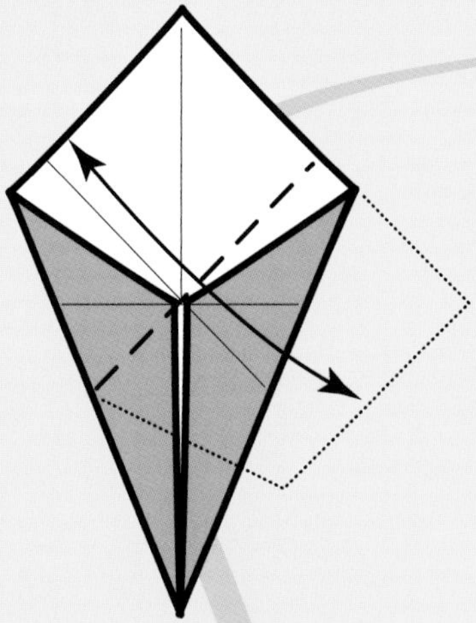

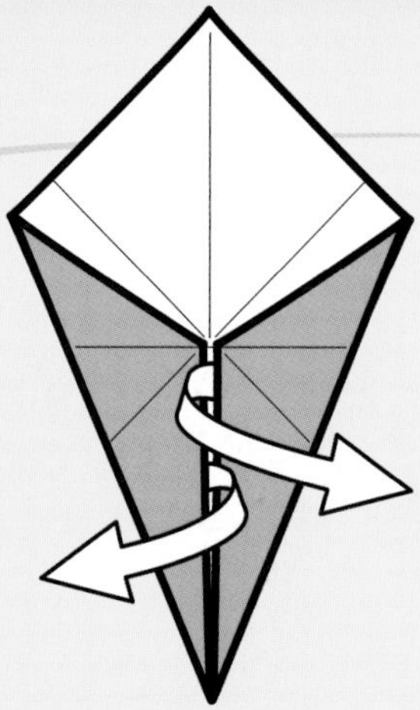

8) Unfold the colored flaps.

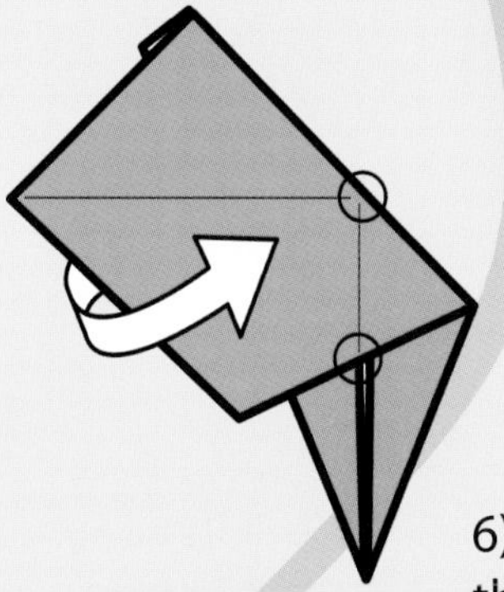

6) Check the creases at the circled points line up as shown, then unfold the last step.

5) Turn the paper over again. Fold the upper right edge downward through the center point (see next drawing)

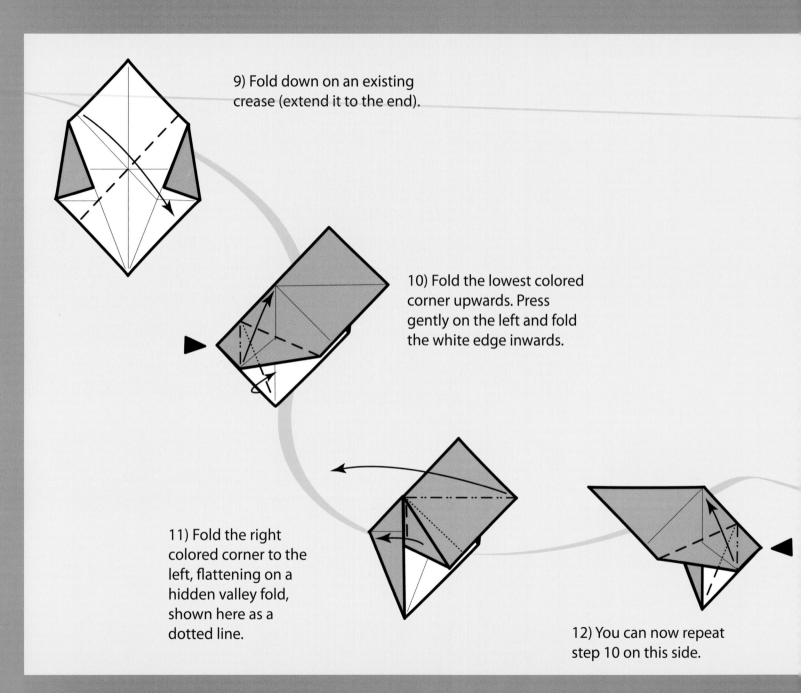

9) Fold down on an existing crease (extend it to the end).

10) Fold the lowest colored corner upwards. Press gently on the left and fold the white edge inwards.

11) Fold the right colored corner to the left, flattening on a hidden valley fold, shown here as a dotted line.

12) You can now repeat step 10 on this side.

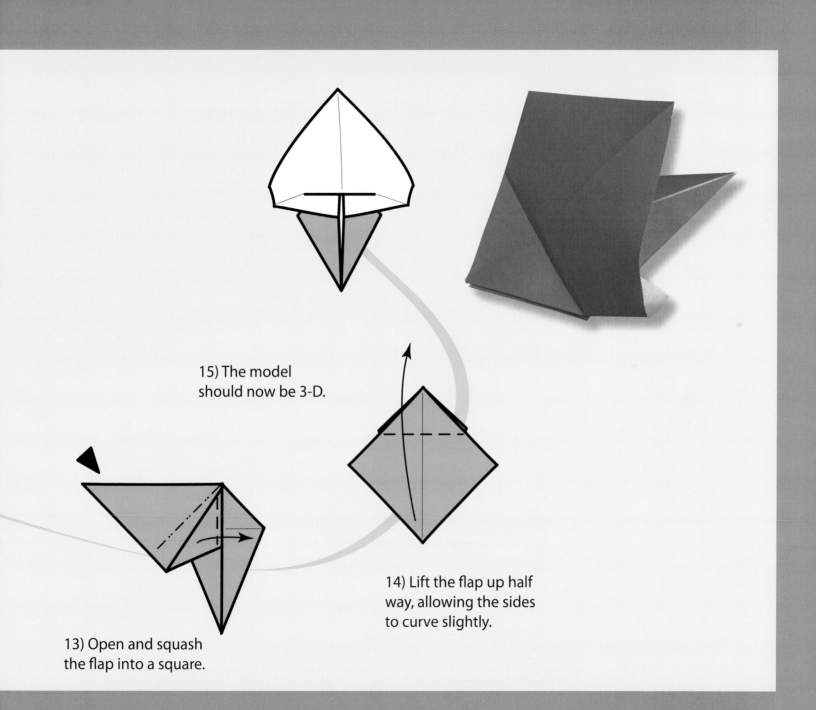

15) The model
should now be 3-D.

14) Lift the flap up half
way, allowing the sides
to curve slightly.

13) Open and squash
the flap into a square.

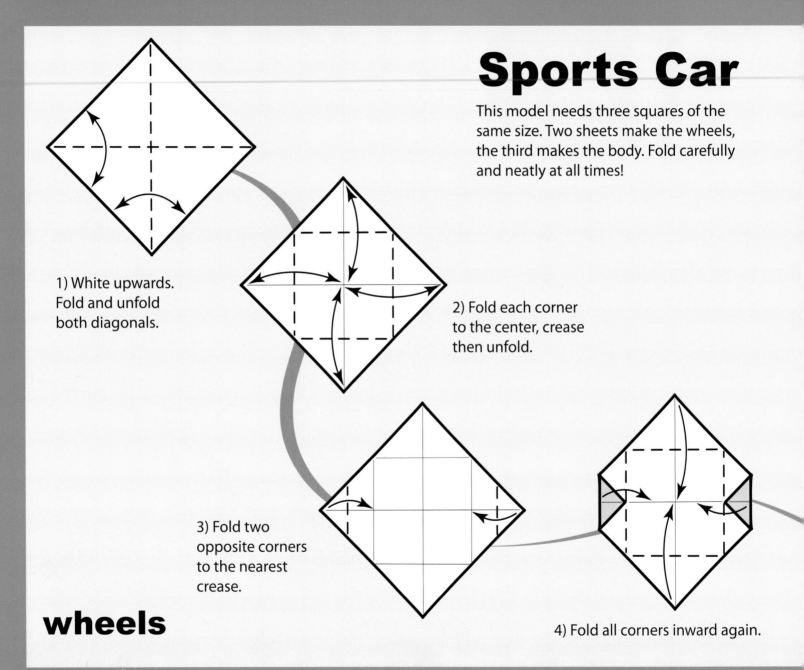

Sports Car

This model needs three squares of the same size. Two sheets make the wheels, the third makes the body. Fold carefully and neatly at all times!

1) White upwards. Fold and unfold both diagonals.

2) Fold each corner to the center, crease then unfold.

3) Fold two opposite corners to the nearest crease.

4) Fold all corners inward again.

wheels

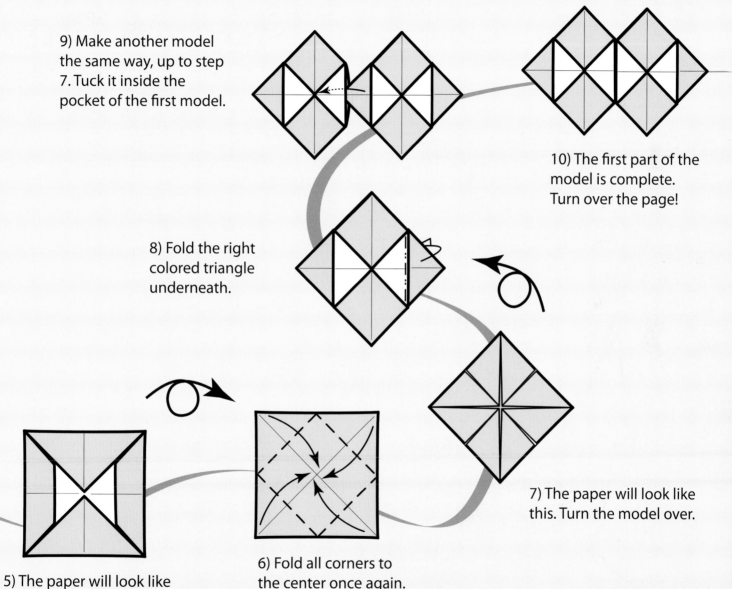

9) Make another model the same way, up to step 7. Tuck it inside the pocket of the first model.

10) The first part of the model is complete. Turn over the page!

8) Fold the right colored triangle underneath.

7) The paper will look like this. Turn the model over.

5) The paper will look like this. Turn the model over.

6) Fold all corners to the center once again.

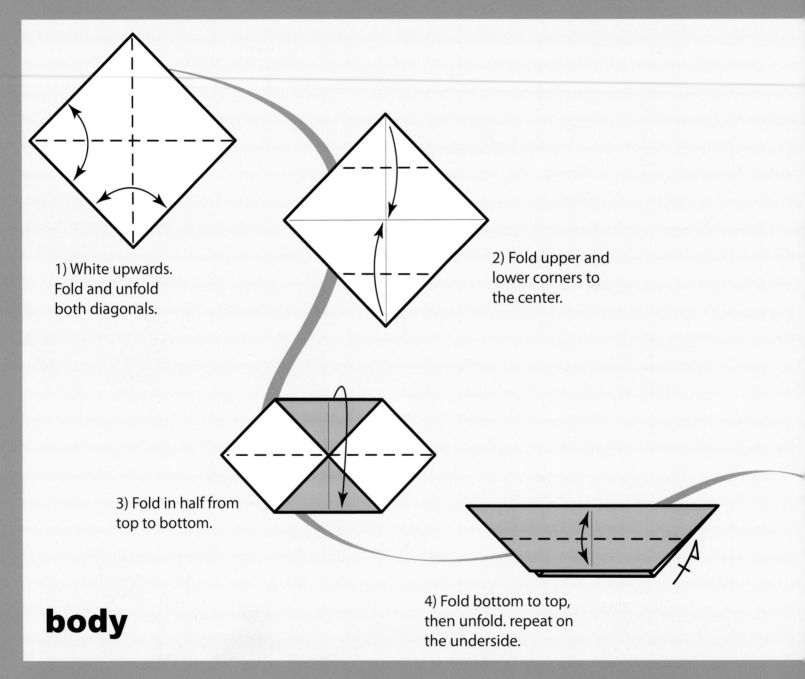

1) White upwards. Fold and unfold both diagonals.

2) Fold upper and lower corners to the center.

3) Fold in half from top to bottom.

4) Fold bottom to top, then unfold. repeat on the underside.

body

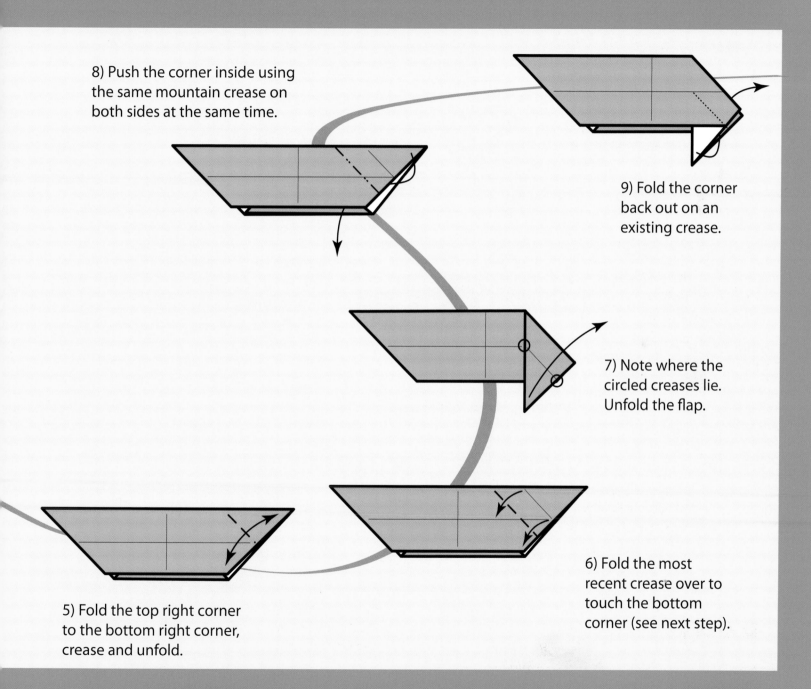

8) Push the corner inside using the same mountain crease on both sides at the same time.

9) Fold the corner back out on an existing crease.

7) Note where the circled creases lie. Unfold the flap.

6) Fold the most recent crease over to touch the bottom corner (see next step).

5) Fold the top right corner to the bottom right corner, crease and unfold.

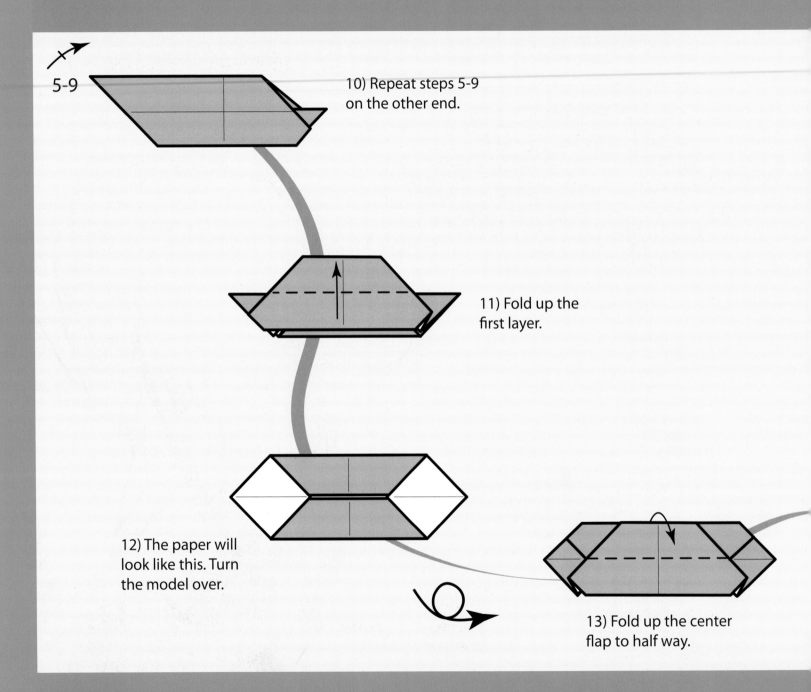

5-9

10) Repeat steps 5-9 on the other end.

11) Fold up the first layer.

12) The paper will look like this. Turn the model over.

13) Fold up the center flap to half way.

3) Fold the sides of the body down and open the wheels out. You decide how 3-D the model should be.

2) Shape the corners of the wheels and fold the corner on the right underneath.

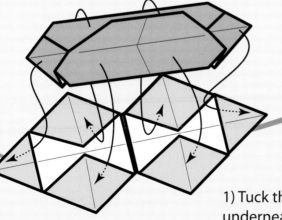

1) Tuck the body underneath the various flaps on the wheels.

assembly

Display Stand

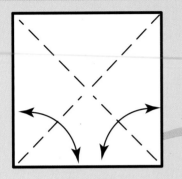

Your models will look even more impressive if you display them on this clever stand. The starting size of paper should have a diagonal just over twice the length of the model.

1) White upwards. Fold and unfold two diagonal creases.

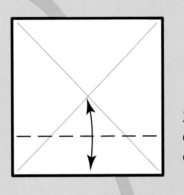

2) Fold the lower edge to the center, crease and unfold.

3) Repeat the last step on the three other sides.

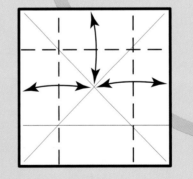

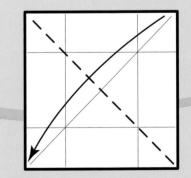

4) Fold the top left corner to the bottom right corner.

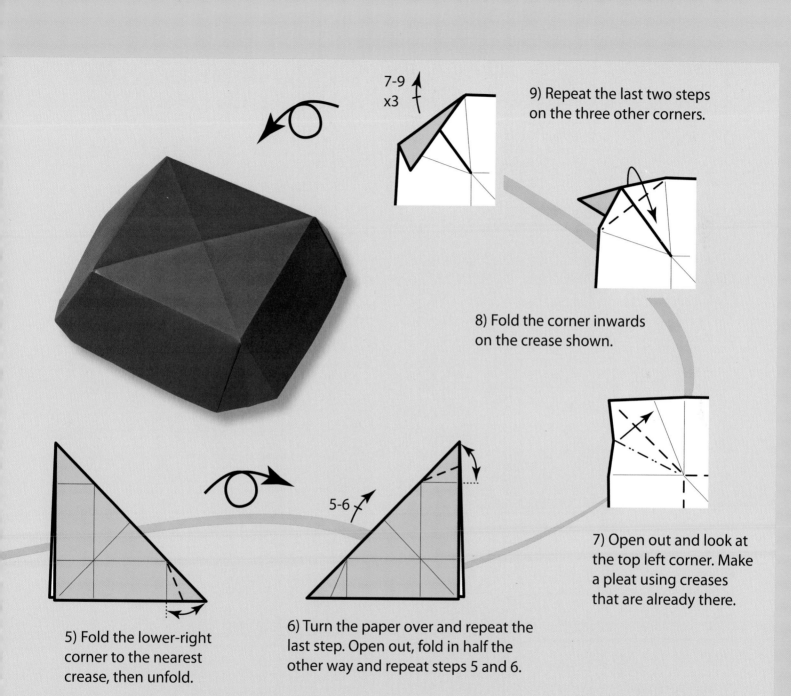

7-9
x3

9) Repeat the last two steps on the three other corners.

8) Fold the corner inwards on the crease shown.

7) Open out and look at the top left corner. Make a pleat using creases that are already there.

5-6

5) Fold the lower-right corner to the nearest crease, then unfold.

6) Turn the paper over and repeat the last step. Open out, fold in half the other way and repeat steps 5 and 6.